MINDSET MASTERY

FOR

ENTREPRENEURS

Leading Experts Share Tips, Tricks,
and Strategies for Success

MINDSET MASTERY

FOR

ENTREPRENEURS

Leading Experts Share Tips, Tricks, and Strategies for Success

DIVYA PAREKH & LISA MARIE PEPE

Get Published

To receive your free gift and see how you, too, can become a published author, email us as getpublishedwithus@gmail.com

Dedication

This book is dedicated to women entrepreneurs across the globe. We are also thrilled to share that the proceeds of the sales of this book (minus our expenses) will be donated to Kiva. Kiva. org is an international nonprofit, founded in 2005 and based in San Francisco, with a mission to connect people through lending to alleviate poverty.

Kiva celebrates and supports people looking to create a better future for themselves, their families, and their communities. By giving as little as $25 to Kiva, anyone can help a borrower start or grow a business, go to school, access clean energy, or realize their potential. For some, it's a matter of survival; for others, it's the fuel for a life-long ambition (Referenced from https://www.kiva.org/work-with-us/fellows).

The profits of this book (minus our expenses) goes straight to Kiva, and once there, 100% of every dollar goes to funding loans. Kiva covers administrative costs primarily through voluntary donations, as well as through support from grants and sponsors.

We can't tell you how excited we are to be supporting lives and dreams in so many lives because of this book!

Divya Parekh and Lisa Marie Pepe

Introduction

Nine incredible women share their best tips, tricks, and techniques for cultivating a positive mindset for sustainable success in life and business. Here you will find stories of overcoming some of life's biggest obstacles that will inspire you to reexamine your own life and the way you view yourself and others. That is the other thing about these nine women – they each work in their own way to empower others to empower themselves and follow their dreams.

That is the central theme that brings these women together. They are dedicated to helping others build a positive mindset. They are dedicated to helping entrepreneurs create success that is born out of having a positive mindset. They have been through trials and tribulations throughout their lives, but they have found a way to emerge stronger each and every single time. Aside from surmounting their own struggles, the nine women writing in this compilation have taken their personal lessons and education and developed a passion for serving others. Being able to share personal anecdotes of one's life is admirable enough; taking it to the next level to reach out a helping hand to others in a similar position speaks volumes to how unselfish these women are.

You will read nine unique passages written by 9 unique female authors. Each author has her own style and her own perspective on what it takes to make it in the world of entrepreneurship! It is instructive to realize that the powerful lessons we discover along the way are often blessings in disguise. Depending on each author's personal journey, you will learn a variety of techniques, all of which will enable you to find the path that is right for you. You may even find that you can relate to one or more of the authors while reading through the various sections of this book.

The title of this anthology, "Mindset Mastery for Entrepreneurs," is quite fitting as it is the central lesson in this book. Most often, we have to learn how to mindfully move away from what we perceive as our struggles, knowing that we are able to overcome them. When we go through milestone difficulties in our lives, often we have to learn how to do things we are not used to doing or even equipped for. This goes for the way we think about ourselves and how we perceive others. When that happens, it is time to take a deep dive and figure out a way to move to rebound. Each of these authors has done just that. Each of their situations was different, and they all dealt with their particular issues in their own way, but collectively they share a common bond that is bound to encourage and excite the reader.

There are many lessons to gather from these stories. Perhaps the most important lesson to learn is about recognizing the relationship between the perception you have of yourself and your level of success. None of the women authors here were satisfied with settling for a life of mediocrity and sitting back after they reached a certain level of accomplishment. They all found a calling of wanting to help other female entrepreneurs create their own success as well. There is a "pass it forward" mentality that should be an inspiration to anyone who reaches a level in life and wonders what to do next. Reach out and lend a helping hand to your fellow entrepreneur.

That is what these nine incredible women did. Enjoy their stories and learn how, you too, can master your mindset for sustainable success in life and business!

Divya Parekh and Lisa Marie Pepe

Contents

"EUDAIMONIA"

A life well lived

Brandy Bonner

Brandy Bonner (The Intentional Woman Author, The Dream Queen) is the Best-Selling Author of books and journals, including The Intentional Woman. She co-authored 1 Word: Discover Reflect & Connect with Words That Can Transform Your Life. She has an amazing story of tragedy and triumph. Brandy is a modern Sojourner Truth going back to rescue others from their nightmares and bring them into the freedom of their Dream Life. She is a powerhouse speaker and empowerment coach for executives and corporations. Brandy produces her own show "Power Talk with The Intentional Woman Author." Her secret sauce is in helping people go "Miles in Minutes" to their Dream Life.

Brandy's favorite pastimes include time with her husband and beautiful daughter, dancing, reading and writing, and living a life of luxury.

You can contact Brandy at theintentionalwoman1@gmail. com. Follow her on Facebook at https://facebook.com/intentionalwomanauthor , or on Twitter at https://twitter.com/dreamqueen113, or on LinkedIn https://www.linkedin.com/in/brandy-bonner-a18634122.

*"A life without our dreams, is a
life beneath our existence."*

Brandy Bonner

The Intentional Woman Author

Hello! I would like to introduce you to a former client named Ann. I changed her name to protect her identity. I met Ann when she was on the verge of a nervous breakdown. She hated her job. Her marriage was on the rocks all the time. She felt that her children were secretly judging her sad, weak, purposeless life. But worst of all, she hated to even look herself in the eye because of the overwhelming shame she felt.

Ann grew up in a house full of abuse and terror. No one was safe at anytime from anyone. Ann's secret hiding place was in her head. She was a prolific and exquisite writer. She could write a grown man into a puddle of his own pitiful tears. She kept boxes full of journals filled with stories, prayers, and heart-wrenching cries for help. It seemed as if no one was ever coming to save her.

Ann was a straight C student. She was brilliant, smart, articulate, and had a photographic memory. She could look at material once and remember it for a test. So why was she a C student? This is where environment trumps everything. When she was at home, it was her job to discern everyone's mood and actions for the day. She was responsible for being the peacekeeper, or as I later termed it, "the Terror Buster." See how much more powerful that feels. That's part of my job as an Empowerment coach, to show my cli-

3

ents their superpowers based on what they have already endured and conquered. Basically, she did not have the time or energy to focus on her studies. And beneath the surface, she had zero confidence in her abilities due to her father's verbal abuse. He told her that nothing she did was ever good enough. Sound familiar?

Let's get back to Ann. Since Ann felt that nothing she did was going to be good enough anyway, she was lackadaisical about everything she did including her school work. She would turn her work in two or three weeks late and her A paper would become a C or D depending on how long she waited or procrastinated. Her teachers could not understand because she was such a good girl, and her writing and comprehension was that of a grown woman. I wonder why?? But Ann became a master at self-sabotage and her best weapon against herself was procrastination. She didn't do anything on time. She did not give her best to anything. Remember, she was taught that her best would never be good enough, so why even try hard or at all.

This spilled over into Ann's college life and eventually into adulthood.

This brings us to where I met Ann two years ago. She had no life in her face. And her world was safely terrifying. She had finally created a safe world for herself. One without risk. One with closed shades. (I could identify with that). A life that had no adventure or perceived happiness at all. Safely terrifying.

I want to briefly walk you through the steps I took Ann through to overcome her self-sabotaging behavior. You would never believe these things about Ann today. She is a take charge kind of woman who gets stuff done. She is a woman that everyone wants to work with. The main compliment she receives now is that she has a stunning work ethic. Ann believes she is responsible for presenting the best of herself at all times.

You too can use these three steps to start to change your own life.

Step 1: Identify the problem and its origin. This may require a trained professional depending on the severity of the situation. Don't worry, I am here for you. I have made a way for you to begin the journey with me, if you so desire. You must discover what is the self-sabotaging behavior and where did it begin.

Step 2: Discover how is this behavior affecting your life? And what is the worst thing that could happen if you don't fix it? The worst thing for Ann is that she was going to live a life that was unfulfilled and never realize any of her talents or dream life. She would never respect herself nor feel like she had earned the respect and admiration she so desired from her husband, children, and community. Ann knew she had to face this self-sabotage head on because a life without her dreams was a life beneath her own existence.

Step 3: Find and execute a solution to the problem. Ann learned to say "Yes" to more opportunities and risk. Sometimes she went overboard, but life was so much more exciting! She learned to immediately get started on any good ideas she had. Whether it was fun, work, family, or risky, she got right on it!! There was way less procrastination. She would create goals and to-do lists to focus on every day. Ann will tell you she is a work in progress, but so much better than she ever knew possible.

Ann is what I would consider a success story. Not because she is living a perfect life now. But because she has taken responsibility for her life and is taking the action needed to create the life of her dreams on a daily basis. And this alone will make anyone a success.

If you would like to know more about my empowerment tools, please feel free to reach out to me on one of the platforms listed above. I would also love to hear how this book has impacted your life and what your takeaways were.

Before I go, please allow me to offer you a Free 30-minute Empowerment Session. I would love to meet you on this journey of transforming your own life. Email me at: theintentionalwoman1@gmail.com to set up your free session.

Take care and remember you deserve to live the life of your dreams. Never rob yourself of that gift again.

Note: Complete the following sections as you deem appropriate.

TAKEAWAYS

What are three things you learned in this section?

_____

_____

_____

_____

_____

_____

_____

_____

_____

_____

_____

_____

_____

_____

_____

_____

_____

_____

_____

_____

_____

_____

_____

_____

_____

_____

EMOTIONS

What are three emotions you experienced in this section?

_____

_____

_____

_____

_____

_____

_____

_____

_____

_____

_____

_____

_____

_____

_____

_____

_____

_____

_____

_____

_____

_____

_____

_____

_____

_____

_____

_____

REFLECTION

How can you use what you've learned in this selection to improve your own mindset?

_____

_____

_____

_____

_____

_____

_____

_____

_____

_____

_____

_____

_____

_____

_____

_____

_____

_____

_____

_____

_____

_____

_____

_____

_____

_____

ACTION STEPS

List 2-3 action steps you intend to follow through starting today.

A CLEARING OF THE MIND & SOUL

Finding my true SELF!

Eva Ponce

Eva Ponce is an Intuitive Life Strategist, Self Care Strategist and the creator of the #CommittedToSelf™ lifestyle and movement.

She helps women figure out where they need to implement self care, who are ready to release chaos and anxiety in order to create a "#CommittedToSelf™ Lifestyle" in their day. Through her results driven strategies, her clients learn how to identify and define their stress triggers along with granting themselves the permission to be their #1 priority by infusing various self care methods into their daily life. She is passionate about women getting back to basics with their health and guarding their energy. Eva, helps them to successfully liberate their lives in order have thriving businesses!

She lives in central New Jersey with her loving husband, her two amazing boys and their fur baby kitty.

Learn more about Eva here: www.evacponce.com and find her as @evacponce on all social media platforms!

Grab your FREE Soul Care Workbook that includes access to her FREE 5 day Soul Care Mini Bootcamp Ecourse delivered daily to your email: http://bit.ly/SoulCareWorkbook.

"We should never stop wanting to grow, learn and evolve to connect to our true SELF."

Eva Ponce

Growing up with a scarcity and lack mentality is difficult to imagine that there anything better on the other side. As a child I was raised with many limiting beliefs. Stories. They all involved money and worthiness.

And by no means was my childhood horrible. My parents raised us the best way possible based on their upbringing. These were their parents beliefs as well. However, these beliefs crippled me as an adult, left me playing small, engulfed me in fear and I internalized the lack to mirror that I WASN'T ENOUGH … It took me over 42 years to realize that this was the background music in mind. These stories were my standard operating procedure.

Fear was my ride or die, not feeling enough was my BFF and scarcity, my silent bully.

In 2015, I quit corporate America to take a chance on becoming an entrepreneur. In this journey, I had uncovered a well hidden pandora's box of money blocks and not feeling ENOUGH. You see your mind dictates your actions. And without soulfully aligned thinking, your actions will always steer you in the wrong direction. It will rob you from knowing that you are capable of change.

It wasn't until I invested in a coach, that we've struck a nerve. Here's when it gets scary, painful and given permission granted to surrender everything I believed as a child. I was confronted with the reality that my MIND was full of unnecessary information that my subconscious used to keep me safe.

Releasing the old and making room for the new...

This where I got curious, hungry for more and did tons of research on mindset, soulset and self-mastery.

I started to cleanse my mind and soul of everything that no longer served me. Along this process I discovered my intuitive, empathic and psychic gifts. In looking back now, I had these gifts all along but suppressed them as child in order to not feel weird or seem awkward. Again, the mind doing its thing to protect me.

Through this transition, I realized I wasn't aligned to my soul. For so many years I was programmed to feed off my old beliefs aka the ego. Not realizing that I could change my thought patterns.

I was able to create a process that allowed me to transform, heal, evolve and serve unapologetically in both my life & business.

I created my own system of "The 5 C's of Soul Care™"

- **SOUL CALLING:** connecting YOU to your purpose

Ask yourSELF: What am I craving to do?

- **SOUL CONSERVATION**: learning how to reserve, refuel, recharge your energy fields

Ask yourSELF: What is my resistance in making my needs a priority?

- **SOUL CONSIDERATION:** taking responsibility for forgiving not only yourself but others for circumstances that no longer provide you pleasure.

Ask yourSELF: What and/or who do I need to forgive?

- **SOUL CEREMONY:** connecting to your higher SELF, creating effective rituals to stay committed to SELF

Ask yourSELF: How can I celebrate myself and bring joy into my day?

- **SOUL CLEARING:** 4 pillars of clear connection; mind, body, soul and environment.

Ask yourSELF: How can I move my body for energy?

How can I clear my mind of negative thoughts?

How can I declutter my environment to feel spaciousness?

How can I fuel my soul today?

In conclusion, know that it takes connecting to your true SELF in order to possess a mindset the serves YOU in your life and especially in your business. Releasing the old beliefs and recreate the new.

Note: Complete the following sections as you deem appropriate.

TAKEAWAYS

What are three things you learned in this section?

_____

_____

_____

_____

_____

_____

_____

_____

_____

_____

_____

_____

_____

_____

_____

_____

_____

_____

_____

_____

_____

_____

_____

_____

_____

_____

_____

EMOTIONS

What are three emotions you experienced in this section?

_____

_____

_____

_____

_____

_____

_____

_____

_____

_____

_____

_____

_____

_____

_____

_____

_____

_____

_____

_____

_____

_____

_____

_____

_____

_____

_____

_____

_____

_____

REFLECTION

How can you use what you've learned in this selection to improve your own mindset?

_____
_____
_____
_____
_____
_____
_____
_____
_____
_____
_____
_____
_____
_____
_____
_____
_____
_____
_____
_____
_____
_____
_____
_____
_____
_____

ACTION STEPS

List 2-3 action steps you intend to follow through starting today.

_____

_____

_____

_____

_____

_____

_____

_____

_____

_____

_____

_____

_____

_____

_____

_____

_____

_____

_____

_____

_____

_____

_____

_____

_____

_____

FROM MASSIVE STRESS TO UNSTOPPABLE SUCCESS

How yoga taught me to rule my world

Jen Ryan

Jen Ryan, a Certified Professional Success Coach, has nearly three decades of business experience in the corporate world and as an accomplished entrepreneur. After many years of trying to be everything to everyone, and still maintain a prosperous career, she was overwhelmed and unfulfilled. Nothing ever felt "good enough." All of that changed, however, when she learned to be present in her yoga practice. When Jen mastered mindfulness on her mat, she realized it could carry over and benefit her business life as well. It is now her mission to teach other women how to thrive in business with less stress.

Jen brings her clients and audience to the present moment. Her ability to meet people where they are is critical to helping them find clarity and build confidence as they achieve massive success in their business and personal lives.

Free PDF Worksheet to get you started. This worksheet will help shift your mindset and get your out of your head so you can get moving with intentions for success. bit.ly/Jenryantips

I am here, arms outstretched and chest heavy. My hands are damp against my mat and I'm watching a woman, about ten years older than myself, lift her body into a headstand. I remember feeling a week ago how that woman must feel right now, my mental and physical strength so in sync. But today I am tired. My shoulders ache. I want to be strong like this woman, and then I realize what I'm doing. I have dishonored myself by letting another person's action shake my perception of my own strength. I close my eyes. Deep breath in. Strong exhale. I bring focus back to my mat. Press into my hands and feet and hear the soft strength of my own heartbeat. I remember that I am enough.

I've had many moments like this. Moments of self-deprecation, of judgement and comparison. Perhaps they come from years of putting too much stock in other people's expectations of me. Perhaps it's a manifestation of the part of me that feels I must fight for everything. But through this journey towards career-fulfillment and self-love, I found a kind of success I never knew was important — success of the self. While there are many steps you can take to discover this, there are three fundamental actions that will not only elevate you personally, but help your business thrive.

Like in any good yoga practice, in life you must first build a foundation. This foundation is built on trust of yourself and is strengthened by people who support and uplift you. While it may seem like an obvious step, it can be hard to admit that people you care about aren't helping you build your foundation. The people that know you the best can sometimes be the most judgmental, and while their intentions may be good, the honest relationship you have with yourself will give you far more guidance than skepticism from others. Let go of the judgements others put on you.

Next, separate from the need to judge them back. When you focus on others, whether negatively or positively, you draw energy away from yourself. The cruelty of comparing your life to others harms your individual growth. You are you. You have strengths and weaknesses that, like a fingerprint, create the original formula of you. To yearn to be someone else is the greatest disservice to yourself and the world around you. You have gifts that others don't. You have experiences and insights and wisdom that others don't. Your value lies in your truth. Seeing who you are in an honest and positive way is one of the most vital steps to cultivating personal success, as well as success in your business.

Finally, you must look inward and be present. How are you feeling? Not this month. Not this week. Not even this day. In this moment, how do you feel? Are you tired? Energized? Peaceful? Manic? Whatever the answer, honor it. Honor the person you are right now, rather than who you were yesterday, or who you might be tomorrow. The only way to move forward is to know where you are now. It is the greatest act of kindness to yourself. Living presently brings clarity, and with clarity comes the opportunity for success in all aspects of life.

What can you do now to start seeing positive changes in your life and business? Start taking stock of the people in your life who fully support you and promote your growth and well-being. The people that build you up when you're feeling your lowest are your foundation.

Next, start making real efforts to stop comparing your life to others' and judging yourself or other people harshly. If you notice yourself doing either of these things, stop, take a breath, and think about why you're doing it. What is causing this comparison or judgement? Is it insecurity? Anger? Start journaling. When you look inward for the answers, your self-awareness will grow, and in turn so will you.

And lastly, when you find yourself overwhelmed with the day or week ahead of you, stressing about life that hasn't even happened yet, pull back. Engage in the present. Start with daily ten-minute meditations. Go for a light walk on a lunch break. Do small things for yourself that will allow you to be in and appreciate the moment. You can't do anything yesterday, and tomorrow never comes, so focus on the now and witness your personal and professional life flourish.

Note: Complete the sections as you deem appropriate.

TAKEAWAYS

What are three emotions you experienced in this section?

_____
_____
_____
_____
_____
_____
_____
_____
_____
_____
_____
_____
_____
_____
_____
_____
_____
_____
_____
_____
_____
_____
_____
_____
_____
_____

EMOTIONS

What are three emotions you experienced in this section?

_____
_____
_____
_____
_____
_____
_____
_____
_____
_____
_____
_____
_____
_____
_____
_____
_____
_____
_____
_____
_____
_____
_____
_____
_____
_____
_____

REFLECTION

How can you use what you've learned in this selection to improve your own mindset?

_____

_____

_____

_____

_____

_____

_____

_____

_____

_____

_____

_____

_____

_____

_____

_____

_____

_____

_____

_____

_____

_____

_____

_____

_____

_____

_____

ACTION STEPS

List 2-3 action steps you intend to follow through starting today.

_____
_____
_____
_____
_____
_____
_____
_____
_____
_____
_____
_____
_____
_____
_____
_____
_____
_____
_____
_____
_____
_____
_____
_____
_____
_____
_____

FENG SHUI OF MONEY

Surround yourself with happiness

Marianna Y. Smith

Marianna Y. Smith is an Intuitive Soul Healer who specializes in personal empowerment and spiritual healing. She uses her gifts and years of experience to craft programs designed to connect others with their inner power, releasing fear and attachments from their lives. Having worked through many blocks and obstacles herself, Marianna is passionate about helping empower others to reclaim the joy, affluence, and freedom that we all deserve. Learn more about Marianna and her programs by visiting her website at mariannaysmith.com or following her on Facebook at https://facebook.com/mariannaysmith888.

The Feng Shui of Money focuses on surrounding yourself with what makes you happy. This free meditation is created to bring in the powerful energy for an abundant spirit animal: The Golden Dragon. Please visit mariannaysmith.com to download it.

"Surround yourself with happiness and your dreams will become reality!"

Marianna Y. Smith

There's so much that can be written, and has been written, about the subject of money, the law of attraction, manifestation, abundance, whatever you call it. It all boils down to: we want it.

We want a prosperous life: the flow, the ease, and everything else that comes with it. But we make it so complicated that we are afraid to chase the dream. You want money, but how do you go get it? Your thoughts, your feelings, your actions are all important in this cycle of life. How we look at money determines which path we take.

Feng Shui is the ancient Chinese art of arranging your surroundings in harmony and balance with the natural world around you. I talk about the Feng Shui of money because I use what makes me happy to make money. In Asian culture there is a statue called Jin Tien (also known as the Money Toad). Jin Tien literally means "money, come to me." The legends say that the money toad likes to sit on a pile of money, so she wants money to come into the house. With her influence you will find things going your way. Suddenly you get clarity, and things just flow.

One of my clients had a $2,000 bill for her son's dental surgery. Together, we meditated with Jin Tien's energy. A couple days later, her ex-husband stepped up to the plate and contacted the insurance company, and she didn't have to pay the bill. She was very pleased, because this never happened before.

The Money Tree is another Feng Shui tool. I love the money tree, whether it's represented by the coins of the ancient Ming dynasty, or by the real money tree plant from South America. The Money tree represents the essence of the Wu Xing, the five elements on earth in traditional Chinese culture: Water, wood, fire, metal and earth. It brings the cycle of life and prosperity into the house, intertwining, creating and allowing it to grow. It's so simple but we never think of it. These thoughts and tools create the flow through the five elements of life and the five senses. That's what I like to have in my house: the Flow of prosperity, the Flow of abundance, the Flow of feelings, the Flow of realization.

Feng Shui is all about balance and flow. Just like life, really. If you want happiness, prosperity, and positive energy to surround you, surround yourself with what makes you happy and clear away the blocks. Visualize what makes you happy. Asian culture makes me happy, so I have the Buddha, bamboo, and Jin Tien sitting in the Feng Shui corner of my house (North West). I have crystals, money trees, and a year of the dog statue with piles of money because is the year of the dog in my office. These items, along with pictures of my family, represent everything that I love.

Looking at life this way affects everyone around you. My daughter is a kind hearted, giving kid. One day I saw her leaving quarters outside stores, on the side walk, in branches, and in front of windows where people would see them. Heads up, of course for good luck! Apparently, she took the money out of her piggy bank before we left. When I asked her why she was doing this, she said it was for other people to find and to have good luck. When I asked why wouldn't she rather take the quarters home and save them, she looked me in the eyes and said, "It will come back to me. I just want to help other people along with me." It was a beautiful moment, I was so proud of her. A few weeks later, she and my husband counted the random change she'd found, and the money earned from doing special chores. She had fifty more dollars than she had before she distributed those quarters. She didn't try to get the money back, but she did tenfold. Now, I'm not suggesting you should start seeding your neighborhood with loose change, but think about the mentality. She wasn't worried about having money because she knew it would come back to her. By helping others, she helped herself.

Your thoughts become your emotions and turn into actions. The energy you put out to the world and the reactions of others is the fulfillment of the circle of life. The Universe provides. Buddha provides. God provides. You just have to figure out what makes you happy. The thought of having money makes you happy because you can go out and buy things, do things, do whatever you want. You give, you thank, you allow.

Understanding and living a blissful life takes practice; not everything happens overnight. People are creatures of habit and it takes time to create a new routine. Training the mind, body, and spirit takes time. Focusing on what you want to come in is the priority, but life happens. Don't make life complicated or try to go against the direction of the flow. Have an idea, create the goal, and go after it. The people that succeed are the ones that stick with their plans and allow them to grow and evolve into the reality of their dreams, or even into something better. Frequently, people give up and chase a different dream, giving up just a second before success is achieved.

Use your surroundings and decide that this is the time for something better. Once you do, everything will flow.

Another client of mine was having issues at work. The work issues affected her health, her well-being, and her relationships with her family. She was afraid to stand up for herself to achieve a higher place of abundance. She had the skills, the knowledge and an idea of what she wanted. But her thoughts were holding her back. She always said, "I don't know. I don't think my supervisors will go for it. I'm nervous that I won't be able to perform in the position." How many of us have had similar thoughts? One day, during a session, we had a breakthrough! She realized that she wasn't in charge of her thoughts and her drive, that her fear was putting obstacles in her way. She began to see life from a point of view of surety, changing to ideas of, "I'm not worried because I know I'm talented, skilled and something good will come my way." Since that breakthrough, she's become more comfortable standing up for herself at work. She also started a side business to support herself so she does not have to rely on the whims of her employer. Her stress level went down, and her health and personal relationships improved. As she relaxed her mind, things began turning in the direction she wanted. She is proof that just a slight change in perspective, a shift focus, can mean wonders in all aspects of your life.

A more personal example, in January of 2017, I decided that I wanted to create an oracle card deck. I went to every artist I could find, trying to find someone who could produce my vision affordably. I started chasing it, but the opportunity did not present itself. When I stopped chasing it and allowed it to come to me, it did! I thought to myself, "You know what? It's going to happen. I just need to keep my eyes open. I am going to put in 30%. God and the Universe will provide the rest." It worked! I didn't have to do anything other than what I already do. I sat down with someone new, with no self-imposed pressure, and explained my vision. I started with my personal motto: I am already at a no; I can only go up from there. We came to an agreement to create a deck together. There it was. If I had continued to chase it, I'd have kept chasing it away instead of attracting it.

The path to abundance, prosperity, and happiness is heavily dependent on what you surround yourself with. Gather the things that make you happiest, including other happy and motivated people. Establish your goals, put forth the effort and think positively about the outcome. It's not a matter of if, but when. Do it with a good mind and a good heart. As the positivity and energy flow to and around you, think, react, feel. Use your five senses with the tools given to you by the ancient wisdom of the world. Then and only then will you succeed.

Note: Complete the sections as you deem appropriate.

TAKEAWAYS

What are three emotions you experienced in this section?

_____

_____

_____

_____

_____

_____

_____

_____

_____

_____

_____

_____

_____

_____

_____

_____

_____

_____

_____

_____

_____

_____

_____

_____

_____

_____

_____

EMOTIONS

What are three emotions you experienced in this section?

REFLECTION

How can you use what you've learned in this selection to improve your own mindset?

ACTION STEPS

List 2-3 action steps you intend to follow through starting today.

MINDFUL, MOTIVATED & MASTERFUL

Why you need a prosperity mindset

Moira Hutchison

Moira Hutchison is a Mindfulness Coach, Tarot Card Reader, and a Spiritual and Metaphysical Healer. She is dedicated to helping people all over the world break free of the invisible barriers that block their ability to live to their fullest potential. Using her own approach – The Letting Go Process – she helps people shift from feeling stuck, overwhelmed, and thinking there must be more to life, to alignment with their life purpose, inspired, empowered, and actually in control of their life experience.

If you are feeling stuck and challenged by your mindset, emotional, and wellness goals, or if you are struggling to figure out your life purpose and are ready to find a deep sense of meaning in your life – Moira will help you recognize what the actual blocks are and then work with you to create a plan of action to get you from where you are to where you wish to be with grace and ease.

http://www.wellnesswithmoira.com/Change-Your-Mindset. htm

"Learning to motivate yourself is more important than any concepts of discipline, motivation, enthusiasm, and willpower."

Moira Hutchison

We hear it so often: "success is a state of mind." Some argue that success is a natural result of proper planning, preparation, and focused action. That viewpoint certainly holds truth — but there are also many exceptions to challenge the "rule." Have you ever wondered how two people can attempt the same objective in the same way and only one of them succeed? Is it sheer luck? Timing? Tenacity? More often than not, it's a person's mindset that determines whether they fail or succeed.

What is a mindset, anyway? Typically, mindset refers to your predominant state of mind on a daily basis. It's what you think about, focus on, and expect from your daily experiences. Think negatively, expect the worst, feel pessimistic about your options, and that's exactly what you will draw into your life. Equally, think positively, expect the best and focus on a successful outcome and you get it most of the time!

Makes sense, right? But how does this work? Why is a prosperity mindset so important? There are three main reasons:

1) A prosperity mindset boosts your confidence and self-belief.

A lack of belief in yourself usually comes along with a sense of powerlessness and futility, which is the exact opposite of a prosperity mindset. Lack of confidence means you see no point in trying to be successful because it won't happen anyway. This type of mindset is a recipe for failure in any endeavor.

Having a true prosperity mindset, on the other hand, means you believe in yourself and your abilities. You believe you can succeed at nearly anything you try, and you are willing to give it your best shot. Even better, the more you do try, the more confidence and self-belief you build — until you are virtually unstoppable!

2) A prosperity mindset strengthens your determination.

Without a prosperity mindset, one failure is enough to convince you that going for your goals is a waste of time. Tenacity and determination don't exist in your world. If you don't become a powerful success the first time you try, you speculate that it was just not meant to be. Unfortunately, few things worth having are achieved so easily!

A prosperity mindset strengthens your awareness that a failure is not the end of the story — it's just something that didn't work out the way you planned. In fact, a true prosperity mindset makes it obvious that the only true failure happens when you stop trying.

3) A prosperity mindset encourages fruitful actions.

Have you ever found yourself wandering in circles because you didn't know the best way to approach a project? Perhaps you had an idea of the best course of action but you felt intimidated by some of the steps. As a result, you may have sabotaged your efforts as you searched in vain for an easier or less scary way to your goal.

With a true prosperity mindset, you will always know the most effective steps that lead directly to your goal. You will have the inner confidence and determination to pursue them — which is a sure recipe for . . . you guessed it: prosperity!!

If I had to sum up how to develop a prosperity mindset into as few words as possible, I'd say this:

Go for your dreams.

Think positively.

Believe in yourself.

Believe you can do better.

Learn, grow and develop yourself.

Be willing to take chances.

Give it your all.

Expect the best in every situation.

Be willing to fail.

When you fall down, get back up and start again.

Keep doing all of this and you can't help but become prosperous and successful, from the inside out.

Note: Complete the sections as you deem appropriate.

TAKEAWAYS

What are three emotions you experienced in this section?

_____

_____

_____

_____

_____

_____

_____

_____

_____

_____

_____

_____

_____

_____

_____

_____

_____

_____

_____

_____

_____

_____

_____

_____

_____

_____

_____

EMOTIONS

What are three emotions you experienced in this section?

REFLECTION

How can you use what you've learned in this selection to improve your own mindset?

_____

_____

_____

_____

_____

_____

_____

_____

_____

_____

_____

_____

_____

_____

_____

_____

_____

_____

_____

_____

_____

_____

_____

_____

_____

_____

_____

ACTION STEPS

List 2-3 action steps you intend to follow through starting today.

_____

_____

_____

_____

_____

_____

_____

_____

_____

_____

_____

_____

_____

_____

_____

_____

_____

_____

_____

_____

_____

_____

_____

_____

_____

_____

_____

_____

SELL OUT TO YOURSELF & YOUR BUSINESS!

Shannon Gonzalez

Shannon Gonzalez is a Spiritual Life Coach and Transformational Medium, she is also a mama, a wife, an author, and a speaker. Shannon helps her clients to awaken and transform their lives by locking into their personal power, selling out to their truth and selling out to success! Shannon is passionate about helping her clients create a life that they truly love living!

Click here https://shannongonzalez.com/sell-out-to-success/ to access a workbook I created to walk you through these strategies.

"Sell out to your personal truth

and sell out to your success!"

Shannon Gonzalez

It's time to sell out to yourself and your business! Your life and your business are only as good as your mindset. Your mindset is really just the stories that you have sold yourself. These stories are often not the TRUTH but are fed by fears, anxieties, and worries.

In this chapter I'll teach you to lock into your personal truth and SELL out to a different story for your life and your business!

When I first started my business, I sold myself stories that were completely false, things that were fed by everything but my actual TRUTH. For example:

1. What if no one likes me
2. What if no one likes or wants to hear my message or buy my product
3. What if I'm not good enough
4. There are so many other people doing what I am doing
5. What if I fail
6. What if I can't run a successful business
7. What if I can't support my family
8. What if I can't make it

Do these stories sound familiar? Let me tell you, we have all been there!

Let me share with you some of the strategies my clients and I use every day to combat these false stories.

1. **Create a daily mindset routine!** Create your own affirmations by turning your negative thoughts into positive statements. For example: When I first started my business, I sold myself that I couldn't be successful running my business and instead had to sell out to what was true. The truth was, that for over 15 years I ran a business so successful, it was one of the highest profiting businesses of its kind in the state. My affirmation was: I CAN run a successful business!

2. **Lock into your vision and purpose!** This is your "why" you do what you do, it is the reason you get up every day. Create a vision board, write it on your wall, on your mirror, or make it your screensaver. Remind yourself everyday what you are working towards and why you want it! This is what will push you when you feel like quitting.

3. **Start each day with a grateful heart!** Take time every day to say or write out all the things that you are thankful for. Include things that you currently have, as well as things that are coming your way. Start your day happy and excited about your life and business.

4. **Show up consistently!** Showing up consistently and taking action daily for yourself and business will build your confidence. Show up even when you don't want to, even when it's not convenient!

SNAP yourself out of it! When your fears, worries, anxieties, and old stories hijack your mindset, use the SNAP steps to help you shift your mindset back to what is true.

S - STOP

N - NOTICE what is not true

A - ALIGN with what is true

P - PRAISE show praise and be thankful for what you have

By applying these strategies, shifting your mindset, and selling out to a different story, YOU WILL SELL OUT TO SUCCESS! Are you ready to for it? Click here https://shannongonzalez.com/sell-out-to-success/ to access a workbook I created to walk you through these strategies.

Note: Complete the sections as you deem appropriate.

TAKEAWAYS

What are three emotions you experienced in this section?

EMOTIONS

What are three emotions you experienced in this section?

REFLECTION

How can you use what you've learned in this selection to improve your own mindset?

_____

_____

_____

_____

_____

_____

_____

_____

_____

_____

_____

_____

_____

_____

_____

_____

_____

_____

_____

_____

_____

_____

_____

_____

_____

_____

_____

_____

ACTION STEPS

List 2-3 action steps you intend to follow through starting today.

_____

_____

_____

_____

_____

_____

_____

_____

_____

_____

_____

_____

_____

_____

_____

_____

_____

_____

_____

_____

_____

_____

_____

_____

MINDSET MASTERY FOCUS FOR ENTREPRENEURS

Susan G. Chamberlain

Susan G. Chamberlain, PhD is a Mystic, Master Intuitive Quantum Healer, Teacher, Coach, and Author ("Holy Quotes from Heaven's Holy Notes" A 365 Day Inspirational Book). She is a Monk in Spirit of Peace Monastic Community & an Ordained Minister in Celebrating Life Ministries for over 15 years. She is a Holistic Practitioner PhD and President of Spiritual Holistic Services. An International Published Article Writer for 'Luminous Women' a Spiritual magazine. She is Host, Director and Producer of 'Spirituality Plus,' a local Staten Island Community Cable Television show. She runs 'Quantum Consciousness' Retreats in Kunkletown, PA. She does Psychic Fairs, Healing Fairs and Workshops at Edgar Cayce Center NYC, where she is a Founding Member.' www.susangchamberlain.com

Free access to my Daily Angel Message. Uplifting Messages to inspire you daily while filling your spirit throughout the day. https://www.susangchamberlain.com/landing-page

"We are wired by GOD for greatness, for prosperity, for abundance; be who GOD created you to be. What you claim, will be your gain."

Susan G. Chamberlain

A ny entrepreneur must maintain a certain mindset mastery for prosperity, being loyal to the energy helps. As an entrepreneur, what energy you have put out in your business you'd like to attract back in with a financial gain and peace of mind that your business is moving forward. You may look to attract a certain group of people or anyone you know who may benefit from your business and its growing field of expertise, all become your target.

You, as an entrepreneur need to keep your focus up along with your business action momentum. The focus should be on your target audience, what their needs are and your products continuous growth to meet the changes of time. Your business action momentum has to be extremely consistent to gain a reasonable and higher than reasonable profit. You must take daily action. If you lose the momentum and drive your business will suffer and of course profits will not reach your target goal.

As an entrepreneur, have love for your business and what you do. You must feel total passion directly in alignment with your heart energy. This passionate energy will drive you and your business forward causing people to attract to you, your field of expertise, your product, your business and your profit. When you create a win-win situation, prosperity is gained on both you and your client or target audience. Passion is an energy that will keep you in a positive momentum as you drive your business forward. You can expect great things with infinite possibilities, when you involve passion into every aspect of your life and business.

Every smart entrepreneur knows about their gut instinct and how important it is to follow it. Smart, wise and dedicated people of their craft and business have this "knowingness" about them and they trust it. As an entrepreneur this is essential, you must trust your gut instinct. Your inner knowingness can advance your business. When you feel it's time to launch your product or change something about your product, trust the feeling. Timing is everything in life. When something is meant to be, trust it and go forward with your proposed intention. Do not hesitate, since the feeling coming in is in alignment with the energy flow; the momentum of your business prosperity.

An entrepreneur using the wisdom of their mind and the passion of their heart in a forward momentum with consistent action, will create consistent results. Remain positive about all things, as there are infinite possibilities of how things can and do workout. A positive mindset leaves no room for negatives or doubt. Trust and faith are an alliance to the well-established entrepreneur. As you incorporate these two energies into your field, organic prosperity is a result.

Have love and appreciation for your money and business, it will grow. Catherine Ponder, "I expect lavish abundance in every way and every day in my life and in my business. Specifically, I expect lavish abundance today."

As an entrepreneur, be mindful of your business, its purpose and how you serve. Be in a constant state of gratitude for yourself, your life and your business. Give thanks for all that you are and all that you have, prosperity is for all of us. Expect miracles in your life and business and they will occur. allow your life and business to grow and expand reaching and surpassing your original goals. When we step out of our comfort zone and allow the universe's energy to work through us miracles, infinite possibilities really do occur.

Author: Susan G. Chamberlain, PhD
Susangchamberlain.com
Ssangchamberlain@gmail.com

Note: Complete the sections as you deem appropriate.

TAKEAWAYS

What are three emotions you experienced in this section?

EMOTIONS

What are three emotions you experienced in this section?

_____
_____
_____
_____
_____
_____
_____
_____
_____
_____
_____
_____
_____
_____
_____
_____
_____
_____
_____
_____
_____
_____
_____
_____
_____

REFLECTION

How can you use what you've learned in this selection to improve your own mindset?

_____

_____

_____

_____

_____

_____

_____

_____

_____

_____

_____

_____

_____

_____

_____

_____

_____

_____

_____

_____

_____

_____

_____

_____

_____

ACTION STEPS

List 2-3 action steps you intend to follow through starting today.

_____
_____
_____
_____
_____
_____
_____
_____
_____
_____
_____
_____
_____
_____
_____
_____
_____
_____
_____
_____
_____
_____
_____
_____
_____
_____

HEALING THE SOUL
TO HEAL THE MIND

Tara Marshall

Tara Marshall is the owner of Healing Spaces Wellness, a local business in suburban Maryland providing reiki healing & instruction, spiritual wellness coaching, women's empowerment workshops, retreats and private events, and healing workshops. As a yoga/meditation instructor, Reiki Master/Teacher, Ordained Minister, divine feminine empowerment advocate, and Spiritual Wellness Coach, Tara has devoted her life to helping others delve deep into their innermost selves to learn that the power to heal themselves rests within. A student of metaphysics since 2010, Tara first studied the ancient healing technique of Reiki at the University of Maryland Center for Integrative Medicine, learning how to incorporate ancient healing techniques in the modern Western world. Since then, Tara continued to build on her healing toolkit, studying with other masters and deepening her healing knowledge in Hana (ancient Hawaiian shamanic) healing, Kundalini Reiki, Crystalline Reiki, DNA Reiki, Karuna TM Reiki, Holy Fire Reiki, Sacred Soul Alignment TM and Akashic Record healing. With her background in meditation and a myriad of healing modalities, Tara also speaks to corporate and private groups, teaching spiritual development and mindfulness as tools of eliminating stress, gaining deeper clarity and meaning in all aspects of life.

Since late 2016, Tara was inspired to reach more women by bringing her healing and spiritual teachings into the online space. You can find her on Facebook at http://www.facebook.com/healingspaceswellness supporting her community, providing intensive masterclasses on a variety of spiritual subjects, and sharing about upcoming events in the D.C. area and around the world.

"While the spoken word is powerful, nothing can shift the mind more powerfully than deep belief."

Tara Marshall

I t was now or never. My twenties lay behind me like a collage of missteps and failed attempts. I had been told to go home. I had been told to return to the land of my birth ... to the womb. I didn't know what "higher self" meant or "divine nudges." I just knew I couldn't fail ... or, to be more accurate, I couldn't admit failure, and going home would be to admit failure. Until the summer of 2012. I knew, then, it was now or never.

I packed up my bags, my children's bags, whatever shambles were left of the life I had created in Maryland, and returned home. My first shift in mindset was finally understanding that, after emerging from years of abuse, I was not failing. I was finally choosing me. Choosing to heal. And I recognized the best place to heal is the place that created me. Upon returning home, I began to read Louise Hay and Wayne Dyer and was introduced to the ideas of affirmations. I thought ... ok, great! I can talk myself into a more positive mindset! I can just tell myself these "positive affirmations" and write these "positive affirmations" over and over and my life will change! While the spoken word is powerful, nothing can shift the mind more powerfully than deep belief. I had to believe those affirmations ... and the truth was, I didn't.

....

I walked into his office ... a makeshift, sterile medical environment that looked exactly like the kind of place that someone like me should be walking into. Someone whose mind was no longer in the driver's seat ... who had all the classic symptoms of depression, anxiety and self-loathing ... who somehow managed to function only because she had to keep her baby alive. I knew a few things at this point. I had escaped the single most abusive relationship in the history of my life. I was now a single mother of two. I had hit rock bottom and there was nowhere to go but up. I also knew that I didn't know where "up" was, or how to get "up," or what was at the end of the journey "up." Despite that, I knew I would find myself there ... in that nondescript place "up" ward from where I was. I would find the life I was meant to live there ... at some point on the journey "up." And here lay my salvation.

I sat down and faced this awkward looking man with the kindest eyes of anyone I had ever met. Kindness was unfamiliar to me, but I knew it when I saw it. During the months that followed, I learned that naming a thing is the first step in healing. I learned that permanence of "things" isn't real, but permanency of the intangible is through legacy. I learned that this entire life experience is meant to be embraced and lived with lots of grace. When I walked into that room, I had the mindset of defeat. I was buried in self-imposed shame and self-loathing about my choices in life. (I didn't care about any of my amazing accomplishments, of course. No, that would be too ... kind.) Every "mistake" was personified as judge, jury and executioner. When I emerged, I knew all that had been burned on the pyre, because I not only encountered my true self, I learned to love her, and I bathed her in the healing balm of self-compassion and understanding. Only through healing my soul from trauma was I able to heal my mind into possibility.

This is for the person who will not let themselves move forward because their mind has held them in the prison of self-judgment and self-loathing. Know that you are not your "mistakes." You are not your life experiences. You are a transcendent being … a living soul creating a flawed, complex, beautiful human life and the only thing that matters, the only thing that lasts, is what you create.

Note: Complete the sections as you deem appropriate.

TAKEAWAYS

What are three emotions you experienced in this section?

_____
_____
_____
_____
_____
_____
_____
_____
_____
_____
_____
_____
_____
_____
_____
_____
_____
_____
_____
_____
_____
_____
_____

EMOTIONS

What are three emotions you experienced in this section?

_____

_____

_____

_____

_____

_____

_____

_____

_____

_____

_____

_____

_____

_____

_____

_____

_____

_____

_____

_____

_____

_____

_____

_____

_____

_____

_____

REFLECTION

How can you use what you've learned in this selection to improve your own mindset?

_____

_____

_____

_____

_____

_____

_____

_____

_____

_____

_____

_____

_____

_____

_____

_____

_____

_____

_____

_____

_____

_____

_____

_____

_____

_____

_____

_____

ACTION STEPS

List 2-3 action steps you intend to follow through starting today.

4 WAYS TO SHATTER SELF-LIMITING BELIEFS FOR WOMEN ENTREPRENEURS

Lisa Marie Pepe

Lisa Marie Pepe is The Confidence Coach & Online Visibility Expert for passionate, heart-centered women entrepreneurs, a #1 International Best-Selling Author of The Art of Unlearning: Top Experts Share Conscious Choices for Empowered Living, and a Motivational Speaker.

Trained at the graduate level in both Education and Clinical Psychology with over three years of experience as a successful Virtual Assistant and Social Media Manager, Lisa Marie empowers her clients to fully embrace their unique gifts and talents by providing them with the skills they need to develop rock-solid confidence and become vibrantly visible online.

She has been featured in The Huffington Post, Thrive Global, YFS, and several other noteworthy publications. Lisa Marie has also appeared as a special guest expert on over 40 international telesummits and has been interviewed on dozens of highly regarded podcasts such as The Stellar Life, The Big Movement, and Women in Leadership.

Lisa Marie is available to speak on self-empowerment, overcoming obstacles, confidence building, positive psychology, entrepreneurship, online business growth and development, and online visibility strategy. For more information or to contact Lisa Marie, please visit her website http://www.positivetransformation.net or email lisa@positivetransformation.net.

"The Empowered Woman's Guide to Thriving in Life and Business"

https://positivetransformationlifecoaching.lpages.co/the-empowered-woman-guide/

"Entrepreneurship is not for the faint of heart. It requires dedication, commitment, and a perseverance day in and day out."

Lisa Marie Pepe

There are many perks to being an entrepreneur. For all intents and purposes, you get to: set your own hours (generally speaking), make your own rules, work from wherever you choose, and be your own boss.

Sounds amazing, right?

Well, the truth is entrepreneurship can be a very rewarding, fulfilling, and lucrative endeavor, but it can also be a very frustrating, overwhelming, and isolating experience too. Self-limiting beliefs can wreak havoc on your life, especially when you first start a business and work hard to become an entrepreneur.

To maintain an optimistic outlook and positive attitude during these times, implementing one or more of these four strategies can be very helpful.

1. Start with an attitude of gratitude.

Keeping a gratitude journal is also an excellent way of practicing gratitude. Ideally, carving out a few minutes at the beginning or end of the day to write down the people, things, and experiences you're grateful for helps to keep things in perspective.

Another option is to simply say, "Thank you!" throughout the course of the day each time you experience something that brings you joy. Taking a hot shower, eating a nutritious meal, or just laughing with a friend are all examples of things one may be grateful for. At the end of a tough day, a little gratitude goes a long way and can change your perspective immensely.

2. Cultivate a positive mindset.

Practice one of the following techniques: prayer, mindfulness-based meditation, or visualization exercises. Sitting quietly with your eyes closed for five to ten minutes a day while breathing in and out deeply is a beautiful way to reconnect with yourself. It's also a practical way to stay focused in the present moment. It gives you a chance to tune out the noise of the day.

During this sacred time, if your natural tendency is to speak to God, by all means, speak to Him. If you find you enjoy listening to uplifting music, listen to music. If you find inspiration through visual imagery, find a space in nature that brings you peace. The whole point is to create a sacred space for yourself each day that helps you to feel grounded.

3. Schedule time for self-care.

Self-care is non-negotiable. Taking time to prepare and eat nutritious meals, getting adequate quality sleep and engaging in some sort of vigorous exercise each day are all examples of self-care. Many new entrepreneurs are hesitant to take time away from working on their business (and with good reason).

An all-encompassing desire to escape an office cubicle and break free from "trading hours for dollars" mentality can make many new entrepreneurs feel overwhelmed. There are an infinite number of daily tasks to complete and determination to be successful (no matter what) sometimes overrides the sensibility to practice self-care. The best way to avoid this common pitfall is to schedule self-care each day and adhere to it as you would any other task.

4. Surround yourself with like-minded people.

Get around positive, like-minded people who share the same vision as you and those who understand the spirit of entrepreneurship. One of the biggest obstacles for new entrepreneurs is learning how to cultivate new relationships with others who understand the journey. In short, it takes courage to venture out on your own and you will encounter your fair share of naysayers. It's incredibly difficult to tune out the negativity, especially if it comes from your immediate family, spouse, or friends.

To counter this, find extended support networks of entrepreneurs both online and at in-person networking events. When you find the right network, stay with it. No doubt these are the folks who will be there to support you every step of the way on your entrepreneurial journey. In short, it takes an immense amount of courage to ditch the status quo, leave the 9-5 behind, and take a deep dive into entrepreneurship. Recognize that challenges, self-doubt, and overwhelm are all par for the course of entrepreneurship.

Practice gratitude, engage in a positive mindset practice, schedule routine self-care, and find or create a tribe of positive and uplifting people who will be there to support you along the way. At the end of a tough day, utilizing even just one of these strategies may be all that you need to refocus, regain your composure, and keep going.

Note: Complete the sections as you deem appropriate.

TAKEAWAYS

What are three emotions you experienced in this section?

EMOTIONS

What are three emotions you experienced in this section?

REFLECTION

How can you use what you've learned in this selection to improve your own mindset?

_____

_____

_____

_____

_____

_____

_____

_____

_____

_____

_____

_____

_____

_____

_____

_____

_____

_____

_____

_____

_____

_____

_____

_____

_____

_____

ACTION STEPS

List 2-3 action steps you intend to follow through starting today.

_____

_____

_____

_____

_____

_____

_____

_____

_____

_____

_____

_____

_____

_____

_____

_____

_____

_____

_____

_____

_____

_____

_____

_____

_____

_____

THE 9 ESSENTIAL RELATIONSHIPS TO CULTIVATE YOUR WILDLY SUCCESSFUL BUSINESS

Divya Parekh

Divya Parekh is an award-winning business relationship advisor, international speaker and 5-time #1 International bestselling author and a writing muse who has had great success with aspiring authors, consultants, trainers, leaders, entrepreneurs, and speakers. Divya's books and strategies have been endorsed by the likes of Brian Tracy, Marshall Goldsmith, Kevin Harrington ("Shark Tank"), James Malinchak (ABC's "Secret Millionaire"), Sherry Winn (Two-time Olympian) and many more.

Divya brings her business expertise and success as an author together to guide others in the writing, publication, and marketing of books that will enhance their professional credentials and propel their business to new heights.

The foundation of Divya's success is that any professional or entrepreneur can achieve their highest goals by building and nurturing relationships. She has helped many people create a thriving business that is joyful and easy to run. Her philosophy when it comes to launching books and careers is that it is all about hearts and hugs — how much you impact and help people with your life and your work!

Divya supports both first time and published authors to turn their unique message into an inspiring movement. She does this by helping them communicate their message through business-focused and personalized book writing. This approach, in turn, positions them as an industry leader, accelerates business growth and increases business profits. Divya's best-selling books, including her newest #1 Bestseller, The Entrepreneur's Garden – The Nine Essential Relationships to Cultivate Your Wildly Successful Business, proves that her concepts reap huge rewards.

As a professional certified coach who has helped multi-million-dollar entrepreneurs, seasoned executives, and non-profit leaders from six continents, Divya is actively working with authors with the same passion. Her proven success strategies have resulted in her clients getting six-figure opportunities, five-figure promotions, media recognition, and to the #1 bestseller list on Amazon.

Please accept my Free Gift: Get Started in A Week-Business Book Writing Challenge

Friends, I get a lot of great questions from clients and people about how to get started to write a book in a faster way — without adding stress and a ton of extra hours to their plate. The questions arise because 81% of people have a book in them. Few ever finish. If you believe that you have a message that will impact others, then I know that your book is needed. Many people are doing things in a way that is ... cumbersome, time-consuming, overwhelming and more complicated than they need to be. So, I've decided to create a No-Cost and Low Effort 5 Day Challenge to help you, a person who wants to share their message, make an impact as well as amplify profits.

Join the few and become an author. It's not that hard. I'll walk you through it in a simple, five-day "Get Started in A Week-Business Book Writing" Challenge at your pace and in the comforts of home. https://success.divyaparekh.com/5daywritingchallenge

Love yourself because you are the person who you have been looking for. Love others because resilient relationships enrich life!

Whether I am speaking, advising corporate clients, coaching business owners, or helping authors to write their books and get published, I believe in a holistic approach to my work that encompasses all aspects of a person's life. For me, now is the perfect time to invite and encourage you to join me both personally and professionally to spread our message. Make your daily purpose one of love and making a difference and you will find the path to a joyous, fulfilled life. In doing so, you will make the connections that unlock and empower aspirational kindness, love and direction within each of your relationships. You will also unleash the creative potential within everyone you touch. You will choose

conscious and loving intention every day, building vibrant friend-
ships, family, organizations, and communities, while influencing
our planet and humanity as a whole. Your love, dropped as peb-
bles in the ocean of your daily life, can be the ripple that changes
not only you but also our world.

"Reveal the masterpiece within you.

The time to take action is now!"

Divya Parekh

MY STORY

My journey to embracing love and relationships as the centerpiece of my teachings began with my liberal upbringing in India. My parents encouraged my sister and me to be forward thinking. They taught us that there were no limiting gender boundaries and helped us realize our full potential.

India is a land of diverse cultures, different languages, religious beliefs, yoga and meditation, compassion, and much more. I grew up with meditation and exposure to cultural diversity at home, school, and in society, so meditating became a way of life rather than a chore. It helped me to dream big, define my vision, lay the groundwork for clarity and purpose, and then start my journey with the discipline to stay the course. When I moved to the United States to continue my education here, it was a smooth transition because students and professors were from different cultures and welcomed me into their world. Because the seed of connectivity was planted in me early in life, I felt like I was one of them, and soon we were arguing the merits of the Yankees versus the Mets.

I am drawn to science, I very much enjoy figuring out how and why things work a certain way. In my biochemistry studies, I learned about the interconnection between body, mind, and intellect. I began my career as a university associate professor of chemistry and biochemistry, splitting my time between leading research efforts and teaching graduate students. I left academia, and entered the world of research labs and biopharmaceutical organizations. There I had opportunities to show my leadership in program management, team leading, process engineering, personnel, and partnership development.

I began to develop a passion for coaching. My unbridled desire to make a positive impact on people led me to believe my true calling in life is to help leaders, entrepreneurs and achievers see their genius, reveal their masterpiece, and craft their message of significance. It led to a merger of my biopharmaceutical career with coaching to develop effective evidence-based leadership and partnership programs. I had the opportunity to work with several pharmaceutical and financial organizations and helped them to achieve the results they wanted. The relationships and connections I build with people is the icing on the cake, making my life more productive and fuller.

Relationships

The substance of everything I teach is that you need to focus on your vision of what you want and that you mindfully develop relationships of significance with yourself and others to achieve it. You might underestimate the power you have to design your life. You might feel stuck in your personal or professional life. I have discovered through my own experience, and by helping others learn to develop the types of relationships I have, that you can achieve professional and personal fulfillment at the same time. These connections allow us to bring more joy, more love, and more freedom to our lives.

A word here on mindfulness. As a definition, mindfulness is a conscious choice of living in the present, guided by value-based decisions and non-judgments. Mindfulness is also living with grace. As we focus on our goals, grace weaves its way into day-to-day activities and relationships.

Mindfulness brings self-awareness without judgment. Knowing yourself is the foundation of authenticity. Non-judgment allows you to be accepting of your strengths and limitations. You are open to finding out about your blind spots and emotional hindrances. You can turn them into assets, driven by the values and support of friends and mentors. Mindfulness makes you want to grow, and allows you to learn from your life experiences — failures and successes alike — while retaining humility.

It is necessary to exercise mindfulness as you explore the relationships you have with yourself and others. Some relationships may be more natural; others might take more effort. Regardless, the more you concentrate and work on a relationship, the easier it will be to integrate into your life. In this chapter, we will explore the nine essential relationships (self, time, money, market, team, partners, death, results, and legacy) that when illuminated in our consciousness, when embraced with grace and mindfulness, give us access to the humility and the potential for resilient altruism that is a prerequisite for sharing oneself with others. These serve as the foundational bedrock for developing relationships and connections with others.

Relationship with Self

You might be saying, "I understand that you need to have relationships with various people to have success in your life's work, but what do you mean a relationship with yourself?"

We do need relationships to do what we want in life. First, we need to have a clear understanding of ourselves before we can do anything. You must be clear on the values and message you share with yourself and others. With clarity, you will be empowered and prepare yourself for the desired outcome. Developing this relationship with self empowers you to speak out and communicate authentically. It is the crucial stepping-stone to developing superb leadership skills.

Relationship with self is the underpinning of your life's joy, freedom, and success. When you let core values and mindfulness be your guiding compass, you:

- Will be able to stand up for yourself without being a door-mat.
- Will be able to forgive others for your sake and take the lessons learned from experiences to grow yourself and others.
- Will increase your self-trust, self-confidence, and achieve peak performance.
- Will, on the whole, build a rock-solid foundation that will weather both good and challenging times with equanimity.

Relationship with Time

One of my coaching clients, Lina, had a misguided relationship with time. She mistook busy for being productive. She couldn't understand how she could work 12 hours a day and not seem to get anywhere. She had started her own software company and was frustrated at the inequity between her daily activity and profits.

As we worked together, Lina realized that time is the most valuable currency of life. The key to understanding a relationship with time is knowing where you are in your life right now, and where your personal and professional life is going to be in the long term. Once Lina's vision for her life became clear, she was able to use her time wisely by minimizing distractions, and taking the RIGHT actions. Her company began to thrive, and she had more free time to enjoy the fruits of her labor.

Relationship with Money

People can have a complicated relationship with money. It is crucial to think about what your relationship with money is, especially when you want to increase your profits substantially. It's great to earn it, but it is better to understand early on how to discipline yourself in its use. What you do with your money is the most critical component of your relationship with it.

Nothing illustrates more of a person's nature than what they do with money, particularly when they have either an extreme abundance or scarcity of it. When you align vision and values with personal and professional life, you can achieve balance. This connection carries over to money. Your money mindset allows you to know what having money means and that money is not evil. It gives you the freedom to be mindfully aware of the present moment while knowing that your decisions and actions determine the results.

Your money mindset is going to determine the league you play in. If you think small, you are going to work with clients who want to play in a minor league, or take opportunities that keep you in your comfort zone. If you believe that there is no limit to your business growth, your efforts will focus on clients who want you to help them grow to the next level. You will also seek out opportunities that will catapult you to unimagined levels. When you bring all your values into your work, your business will grow exponentially.

Relationship with Market

The relationship with money motivated me to understand my market. Knowing your market is essential whether you have your own business, or are an executive in a large corporation. We all have a market depending on our business niche. Relationship with the market is knowing and understanding your ideal client, establishing your brand, making a positive impact, and serving your clients to help them succeed in their personal, professional, and financial goals. By aligning yourself with your market, you can provide the best solutions for your clients in your area of expertise.

I have had more than one client who felt like they were spinning their wheels trying to grow their business. Many times, the solution was to help them realize their company did not know or understand their customers well. I helped them build a loyal customer base by shifting their shotgun approach of trying to be everything to everybody to one of connecting and forming relationships with those who could benefit the most from their products or services.

Relationship with Team

When you work with people to achieve a common goal, a healthy relationship with your team is essential. Within a team, the leader is the catalyst that drives his or her team to thrive, so each member provides extreme value both individually and collectively. If you are the leader of a team, you are responsible for strengthening the relationship among the team members.

When I work with organizational or business teams, I help them become high performing teams with humanistic values. The focus is on purpose, encouragement, real-time feedback, and reinforcing structures. Happy team members play a significant role in each other's personal, professional, and financial success because they help accomplish the team's and the company's goals. When you work as a collaborative team, everybody is involved in planning, designing, developing, and implementing those goals. When you achieve the goals, the entire team cheers and celebrates. After all, they helped make it happen!

When you have a connected team, the contributions and support enable you to orchestrate productivity, innovation, creativity, and the best quality products and services. This profitability enhances everyone's life.

Relationship with Partners

Business is a system in which all parts and processes contribute to the success or failure of the whole. We all work with other professionals outside of our organization or business. These specialists or contractors help us with various aspects of our company. You might want partners who share in every aspect of your company from the initial establishment to sustainable success, or the purpose may be to work together for one particular project. The partner could be someone who specializes in a different industry than yours, but his or her company complements yours perfectly because they bring a different perspective to business operations. By joining forces, you grow together.

Whatever your intention is with a partner, it is important to realize that it is about collaborating, not competing. You are pooling resources of the mind and heart. With your partner, you want to create more opportunities, create more emotional and financial wealth, and go beyond what you can do alone. It also means that you sometimes need to have difficult conversations if you have people who are not keeping up their end of the bargain.

For example, I formed a partnership with a book publisher, and we put together a written contract. The contract defined clear expectations including roles and responsibilities of both parties. However, the publisher failed to deliver their end of the agreement. After several unsuccessful attempts to salvage the relationship, I decided to cut them loose. Sometimes, working on a relationship with a partner involves limiting your losses before things become irreparable.

Relationship with Death

As they say, nothing is certain except death and taxes. Our 21st century society tries to insulate us from death. However, proximity to death or failure forces us to explore our fears and feelings about the subject. Doing so gives us the opportunity to live our lives in a new and fulfilling manner.

This relationship is about accepting fear, working through it, and using the grit that you have deep inside of you to overcome it. It is about living life rather than passing through it. Shakespeare said, 'A coward dies a thousand times before his death, but the valiant taste of death but once.' By establishing your relationship with death, you learn to live with that fear in your life. It will help you overcome challenges, go after new opportunities, and set your affairs to take care of your loved ones and your business in the event of your death.

Relationship with Results

Your relationship with results matters! Results are the milestones that tell us if we're going in the right direction. Success requires destination and destination needs direction. Life is a journey comprised of many goals. It is about living a mindful life driven by value-based decisions, learning, unlearning, and relearning while having fun. The relationship with results is how you measure success, clearly defining outcomes, determining progress, and learning from failures as you work toward your goals.

This relationship can take on many forms. I have worked with people who did not know how to handle their success. They didn't know what to do with it, how to continue it, or how to leverage it into significant positive results. Think of that as you get closer to achieving your goals. Are you going to know what to do once you get there?

I had issues with my results when starting out in my coaching career. I was working with great clients and having a degree of success regarding activity and income, but I wasn't happy with it. I evaluated my business growth and mindfully applied the lessons learned from successes and failures. This helped me scale up my business. I went from coaching individual clients to coaching teams and departments in bigger companies. Being comfortable in the relationship with my results allowed me to speak to several hundred people at once and write books to help many others.

Relationship with Legacy

Finally, there is the relationship with legacy. Usually, when we think of a legacy, it is what we leave behind after we leave this world. We all like to believe others will remember us because of what we will leave behind. This is true to an extent, but you can start your legacy NOW! Empowerment has a ripple effect. Your fiery message can ignite a passion in someone else. Every time you act as a leader with your message, you enable others to choose challenges with courage.

There is so much you can do today that will leave an impression on someone's future. It might be working with kids or seniors or animals. It can be working with a local nonprofit or being on the board of a national organization. You never know when giving of yourself is going to impact a person's future. You might not even know them personally, but your efforts could change someone's life forever.

My Legacy

Part of what I teach others and advocate in my own life is creating a sustained solution. I donate a portion of my books' profits to KIVA (Kiva.org). It is an international nonprofit connecting people through lending to alleviate poverty. By giving as little as $25 to Kiva, anyone can help a borrower start or grow a business, go to school, access clean energy, or realize their potential. For some, it's a matter of survival; for others, it's the fuel for a lifelong ambition.

I take a great interest in the lives of our youth. I do not look at it as a cliché but as truth: Children are our future. In some places, our youth have limited access to educational opportunities that could shape their lives and community for the better. I prefer to partner with organizations that take a systematic approach to address root issues rather than slap a Band-Aid on a problem. So, I partner with TMT Youth Community Foundation, a nonprofit organization that focuses on accessing, developing, and growing the talents of young people. I also partner with The Little Maker's Academy that focuses on collaborative learning and critical thinking with young students through hands-on STEAM activities.

I also work with Inspire NC, a student-led non-profit organization whose aim is to promote interest, knowledge, and involvement in the fields of STEAM and develop leadership in the next generation. Through Inspire NC, I mentor a Robotics Team. These young people build and operate robots. They have fun doing it... I don't know how many of them will become great scientists or engineers in the future, but I know what I do is having an impact on their lives.

My work with relationships is one of my legacies, and I take seriously the contribution I make to others' lives. I believe that when you make a difference in your life, a loved one's life, or someone else's, one blends into another. When you are confident in your passion, you work at it. I have a passion for making a difference. I want to reach out and genuinely help others. I find opportunities to do that every day whether it is something small or a larger endeavor. Let this Valentine's Day become the springboard for empowering love in your and others' lives every day.

Live the Life You Want
Grateful I am,
For who I am.
Today, I am,
Ready to take on tomorrow.
When I look back on today,
I have no sorrow.
Right or wrong, choices I will make,
Every day, for my sake
Action over inaction
Purpose, pain, and passion
Learnin to unlearn and relearn
Prepared for what awaits me,
Around every corner, I turn.
Support each other,
and grow together.
Build relations
And bridge nations.
Live your legacy.
There's no fallacy.
Achieving success, happier than ever.
Reducing our stress in this joyful endeavor.
The future is now our present.
Nimbly unwrap your return on investment.

Note: Complete the sections as you deem appropriate.

TAKEAWAYS

What are three emotions you experienced in this section?

_____

_____

_____

_____

_____

_____

_____

_____

_____

_____

_____

_____

_____

_____

_____

_____

_____

_____

_____

_____

_____

_____

_____

_____

_____

EMOTIONS

What are three emotions you experienced in this section?

_____
_____
_____
_____
_____
_____
_____
_____
_____
_____
_____
_____
_____
_____
_____
_____
_____
_____
_____
_____
_____
_____
_____
_____
_____
_____
_____
_____
_____

REFLECTION

How can you use what you've learned in this selection to improve your own mindset?

_____

_____

_____

_____

_____

_____

_____

_____

_____

_____

_____

_____

_____

_____

_____

_____

_____

_____

_____

_____

_____

_____

_____

_____

_____

_____

ACTION STEPS

List 2-3 action steps you intend to follow through starting today.

_____

_____

_____

_____

_____

_____

_____

_____

_____

_____

_____

_____

_____

_____

_____

_____

_____

_____

_____

_____

_____

_____

_____

_____

_____

_____

_____

_____

Will You Leave a Book Review?

Did you enjoy this book and find it useful?

We will be very grateful when you post a short review

and give your success story on Amazon right now!

Your support makes a difference. We read and

respond to all the reviews personally to make this

book even better!

To leave a review right now, go to https://www. amazon.com/

www.ingramcontent.com/pod-product-compliance
Lightning Source LLC
Chambersburg PA
CBHW032007190326
41520CB00007B/391